Getting Around

By Boat

Cassie Mayer

www.heinemann.co.uk/library

Visit our website to find out more information about **Heinemann Library** books.

To order:
 Phone 44 (0) 1865 888066
 Send a fax to 44 (0) 1865 314091
 Visit the Heinemann Bookshop at www.heinemann.co.uk/library to browse our catalogue and order online.

First published in Great Britain by Heinemann Library, Halley Court, Jordan Hill, Oxford OX2 8EJ, part of Harcourt Education. Heinemann is a registered trademark of Harcourt Education Ltd.

© Harcourt Education Ltd 2006.
First published in paperback in 2007.
The moral right of the proprietor has been asserted.

Editorial: Tracey Crawford, Cassie Mayer, Daniel Nunn, and Sarah Chappelow
Design: Jo Hinton-Malivoire
Picture Research: Tracy Cummins
Production: Duncan Gilbert

Originated by Chroma Graphics (Overseas) Pte. Ltd
Printed and bound in China by South China Printing Company

13 digit ISBN 978 0 431 18222 3 (hardback)

11 10 09 08 07 06
10 9 8 7 6 5 4 3 2 1

13 digit ISBN 978 0 431 18319 0 (paperback)

11 10 09 08 07
10 9 8 7 6 5 4 3 2 1

British Library Cataloguing in Publication Data
Mayer, Cassie
Getting around by boat
1.Ocean travel - Juvenile literature 2.Shipping - Juvenile literature 3.Inland water transportation - Juvenile literature 4.Boats and boating - Juvenile literature
I.Title
387

Acknowledgements
The publishers would like to thank the following for permission to reproduce photographs:
Corbis pp. **4** (Lester Lefkowitz), **5** (Frans Lemmens/zefa), **6** (Charles & Josette Lenars), **7** (Chris Lisle), **8** (Onne van der Wal), **9** (Setboun), **10** (Tom Stewart), **11** (Xiaoyang Liu), **12** (Owen Franken), **14** (ML Sinibaldi), **16** (Royalty Free), **17** (Onne van der Wal), **18** (Tom Stewart), **19** (William Manning), **21** (Rob Howard), **23** (fisherman, Tom Stewart), **23** (barge, Charles & Josette Lenars), **23** (motor boat, Onne van der Wal), **23** (ferry boat, Xiaoyang Liu); Getty Images pp. **13** (Streano), **15** (Frerck), **20** (Puddy), **22** (ImageDJ).

Cover image of a river boat reproduced with permission of Hubert Stadler/Corbis. Backcover image of a barge reproduced with permission of Charles & Josette Lenars.

Every effort has been made to contact copyright holders of any material reproduced in this book. Any omissions will be rectified in subsequent printings if notice is given to the publishers.

The paper used to print this book comes from sustainable resources.

Contents

Getting around by boat

Every day people move from place to place.

Some people move by boat.

What boats carry

cargo

Some boats carry cargo.

Some boats carry passengers.

How boats move

Some boats use motors to move.

Some boats use wind to move.

Who goes on boats?

captain

A captain steers the boat.

Passengers ride on boats.

Types of boats

wood

Some boats are made of wood.

steel

Some boats are made of steel.

How people use boats

People sell food from boats.

People catch fish from boats.

Some people ride in boats for fun.

Some people race boats.

Boats can take you out to sea.

Boats can take you into a city.

Some people ride in boats
all alone.

But it is more fun
with friends!

21

Boat vocabulary

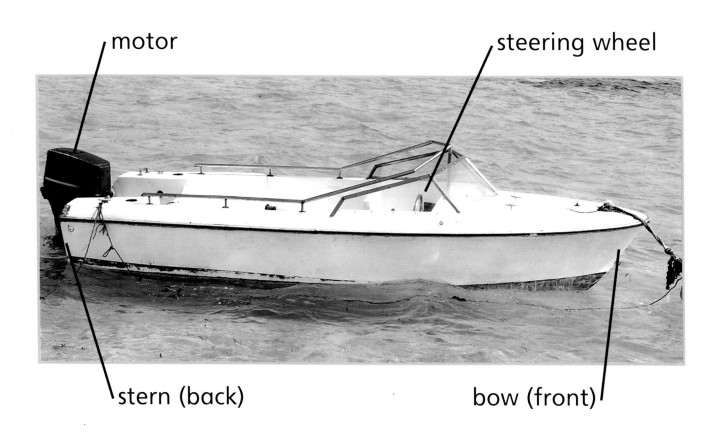

motor

steering wheel

stern (back)

bow (front)

Picture glossary

 **captain** a person who drives a boat

 **cargo** things taken from one place to another

 **motor** engine that makes a boat move

Index

Notes to Parents and Teachers

Before reading

Talk about going on a boat. Where did they go? Where did they sit? What did they see?
Talk about the motor, the stern, the bow, and the steering wheel.
Talk about different sorts of boats e.g. rowing boats, canoes, pedaloes,
sailing boats, ferries.

After reading

Make a simple sailing boat using a foil dish. Shape it with a pointed front and a flat back.
Press a ball of playdough into the centre of the boat. Cut out a triangular sail from
coloured paper and fold in half. Make two slits – one near the top and one near the
bottom of the fold. Unfold the sail and thread a thin straw through the holes. Stick the
mast into the playdough. Watch the boat sail across a washing up bowl of water.
Share the rhyme: "A sailor went to sea, sea, sea. To see what he could see, see, see, But all
that he could see, see, see, Was the bottom of the deep blue sea, sea, sea."
Join in the actions to the rhyme: "Row, row, row your boat, gently down the stream.
Merrily, merrily, merrily, life is but a dream."